Change of heart

Change of heart

a couple's guide

to

relationship transformation

paul & jennifer thibeault

Advantage™

Published by Advantage, Charleston, South Carolina.
Member of Advantage Media Group.

ADVANTAGE is a registered trademark and the Advantage colophon is a trademark of Advantage Media Group, Inc.

Printed in the United States of America

ISBN: 978-1-59932-019-9

Most Advantage Media Group titles are available at special quantity discounts for bulk purchases for sales promotions, premiums, fundraising, and educational use. Special versions or book excerpts can also be created to fit specific needs.

For more information, please write: Special Markets, Advantage Media Group, P.O. Box 272, Charleston, SC 29402 or call 1.866.775.1696.

dedication

We thank God for the blessing of our miraculous transformation.

In loving memory of James Van Law, Sr., the impression you left on our souls is profound. Your presence is continually felt in our lives and was most certainly felt when we needed you most.

table of contents

acknowledgements

We are so grateful to those who have shared their gifts with us as we recreated our relationship. Change of Heart would not have been possible without your love and support.

Tony and Sage Robbins, your compassion and wisdom has changed our lives forever.

Brian and Janet Moses, your strength, honesty and perspective was the ultimate gift of tough love. We will never forget what you have done for us.

Judy Osuna, the energy you gave to our dream while it was just a tiny seed is appreciated more than you will ever know.

Ann McIndoo, your talents, resourcefulness and wonderful personality made our dream a reality. We appreciate your patient guidance. It is a privilege to know you and a joy to have worked with you.

introduction

Our purpose in writing *Change of Heart* is to convey a message of hope and inspiration to married couples who believe that separation or divorce is the only answer because they don't see a way out of the pain, frustration, anger or hurt they associate to their relationship.

For many years, we had the same belief. We felt there was no escape and simply had to tolerate the negative feelings we felt in our marriage. We knew we loved each other but believed we no longer could make each other happy.

We imagine there are many couples searching for the keys to unlock their own self-imposed emotional prison. If you have felt your relationship suffer because of dishonesty, self -esteem, controlling partners or the strain in balancing parenting, work, and extended family with time for each other, we know how desperate this can feel.

If you have spent night after night with your backs to each other, but miles apart emotionally, disconnected and craving the intimacy you once had, we invite you to embrace the idea that you have everything you need within you right now to transform your relationship to everything you desire.

It is possible for you to radically change how you experience your relationship as it was for us. We believe that when you hear the perspective of a couple who has shared so many similar challenges and has made it to the other side, you will be given the inspiration and hope you need to decide what will work in your own relationship.

Our hearts go out to everyone who comes in contact with this book. Our hope is that the ideas expressed in the pages that follow will create an emotional shift within you that will be the catalyst for reigniting the passion you once felt.

With loving hearts,

Jennifer and Paul Thibeault

$$\boxed{1}$$

your emotions are your life

When you are having relationship problems, all different kinds of emotions blend together into a seemingly endless mental loop of pain. Because relationships are so central to many people's lives when they become dysfunctional often the routine of life seems to lose meaning. If you've experienced severe problems with a partner you know it doesn't feel good, but it can be difficult to put your finger on exactly why you feel the way you do.

It might be helpful to know that there are specific thought processes that we engage in consistently that cause us to reinforce negative emotions such as loneliness, insecurity, anger, resentment, desperation, guilt, sadness, hurt and failure. Most people who are living with extreme negative feelings will have a tendency to intensify these emotions in their heads. The feelings become like ocean waves during a storm each wave stronger than the last. The more they become repetitive thoughts, the worse we feel about each other. Not surprisingly, by harboring these disempowering emotions on a regular basis, we tend to get more of what we are telling ourselves we don't want in our relationship. We focus on how lonely we are and how sad that makes us or how angry we are and how much we resent the way we're being treated. That deflates the energy level of our relationship causing us to not want to relate to each other, which only serves to deepen our hurt and disconnection.

Many times couples throw up their arms in desperation feeling like the future will only be filled with more of these painful feelings without realizing that they are not bringing empowering emotions to their problems. They are too close to the tree of their pain to see the forest of their choices.

We'll share tools that we learned to combat these destructive thought patterns and help you gain clarity on what is really tearing your relationship apart. Once you have clarity, you'll feel empowered to reshape your current relationship to that of your desires.

When we learned these powerful tools, we realized that all along we had the choice of which thoughts and emotions we needed to feed our relationship with to experience more joy together. By making the distinction that we actually choose the emotions we allow to dominate our daily existence, we were able to make a conscious decision to feed our relationship with empowering emotions such as love, honesty, faith, patience, courage, optimism, trust and commitment. Since we have chosen to create a life together based on consistently reinforcing positive emotions rather than negative ones everything we thought possible in our relationship has come true.

You may think this is easier said than done or that you don't feel any of these positive emotions for your partner and don't see how you ever could. We can definitely relate; that's exactly how we felt.

Usually, when we are feeling badly toward our partner, we're mostly focused on what we're not "getting out "of the relationship. We reinforce in our heads what he or she is not giving us, which makes us pull back and stop putting energy into the relationship. The fact is, *a relationship is a place you go to give your love and gifts to your partner not to get whatever you can.*

If you focus on figuring out what it is that your partner needs or wants, and focus your energy on delivering that to them, very often you will find they will naturally want to give back. If you want different emotional experiences to start showing up with your partner, it is critical to put in the effort to attract what you desire. Remember, *you only attract what you truly have become in your soul.* When you begin to give, without checking to see what you are getting, things start to turn around.

Questions to Ponder | *Chapter 1: Your Emotions are Your Life*

1. What negative emotions have you indulged too often lately that caused you to feel disconnected from your partner? (Anger, frustration, criticism, spitefulness, loneliness, depression)

2. If you were 100 percent honest with yourself, what do you know you're not giving to your mate that they need? Why are you not giving it?

3. Do you really believe your mate doesn't care about you or could they just be hurting too? What could your partner be hurting about?

4. When you are feeling negative about your relationship, what do you usually do or say? Does that make things better between you?

5. If you were to stop doing what you know hasn't worked, what could you try that might bring you closer together?

6. Does your tone convey love when you speak to each other? What else could your tone be communicating to your mate?

7. What would you have to believe about your partner to feel more excited to be with them?

8. Who do you need to become to create more positive energy together?

9. What does your partner need most from you?

10. How would giving what your partner needs most make them feel toward you? How would it make you feel to know you could satisfy your mate's deepest need?

11. What emotions do you consistently feel in your relationship?

2

is your relationship worth fighting for?

B efore you commit to taking another shot at repairing your relationship, it is important to get in touch with how much of your life's energy has already been absorbed by disappointing efforts to make changes that seemed to end up unappreciated *or unreciprocated.*

How many times have you made efforts to strike up a conversation when your spouse was staring blankly at the television paying no attention to you? Can you remember times when, in spite of feeling unappreciated, you made a gesture of love or giving to your spouse only to be rejected one more time? It is important to appreciate the degree to which those kinds of experiences condition you to believe nothing will ever change that your partner does not care anymore.

You owe it to each other to stop wasting your life together and be completely honest before investing more precious time. What is the bottom line? Are both of you 100 percent committed to making the most of your relationship? Is it possible that you are both scared to call an end to a relationship where you were never right for each other to begin with?

If you have the courage to face the brutal truth, though it may be painful, at least you are both being fair to each other in not allowing one person in the relationship to continue giving while the other hangs on out of convenience or fear of change. Both of you could have a chance at a more fulfilling relationship. You have to honestly answer the question: ***do you really love your spouse?***

We fully understand and respect that there are couples for whom separation or divorce is the right option. Our message is not for those people, but for couples who know in their hearts there is honest, true love between them though they don't feel it the way they once did.

These struggling couples, who know there is real love between them, are usually having trouble feeling that love because of the memories of their past disappointments, hurts, and frustrations. The problem lies in that they are shut off from the true feelings that rest in their hearts. When your head is hijacked by past or present painful memories, your heart is closed.

The reality is that your heart knows the truth and will only guide you when it is open and you are open to its unquestionable intelligence. Most people never take the time to take some deep breaths, be silent for a moment, and ask themselves: What do I really feel is upsetting me? What is the truth about who my spouse is to me? If you could take the step to clear your mind and get in touch with what you really appreciate about your partner you could then build your relationship from a place of truth and love. Questions will direct your focus. While you're in the silent space of your heart's guidance ask questions like: What caused me to fall in love? What has my partner done that has made me feel special? What made my heart feel warm when we were first together? When you first fell in love you were not caught up in your head, so loving feelings naturally flowed. Your relationship began in your heart and only there can it die. **If there is true love still alive, it will not die.**

Once you are in touch with the truth of your feelings toward each other, you must be careful not to judge your future together based on past behavior patterns. It's important at this point, not to repeat the mistakes of the past, which is easy to do if you focus on what you're lacking. No matter how long you've been together or how conditioned you've become to expect unacceptable or inconsiderate treatment things can change. But you have to leave the past in the past as hard as that may be. When you drag the past into your efforts to show more love to each other you will kill the young seeds of change in your relationship.

When we turned our relationship around we had a fifteen year history of learned behavior to counteract. The momentum had shifted in favor of getting a divorce. Near our breaking point, we were both starving for love. When we shifted our focus toward giving each other as much love as we could versus withholding it out of anger or hurt we rejuvenated and expanded the love that always existed between us.

To make the kind of shift we are talking about is a total departure from the paradoxically comfortable ways you have come to treat each other. Even though the quality of your relationship may presently violate things you value such as honesty, trust, intimacy, tenderness, thoughtfulness, and fun, you may have grown comfortable in accepting the current state of your relationship. What you have to ask yourself is: Are you willing to get uncomfortable enough with the routine of your life to break out of the rut you've created together? We have found the most uncomfortable experiences we put ourselves through were things like facing the truth of how we had chosen to consistently treat each other, having the courage to take responsibility for our actions, and having the faith in each other in spite of our past that we would nurture our relationship much more lovingly in the future. Unless you have a willingness to do whatever it takes to make a dramatic shift in your relationship, your changes will be temporary and soon you'll slide back to your old ways.

Questions to Ponder | *Chapter 2: Is your relationship worth fighting for?*

1. What are the core qualities of your partner that attracted you initially?

2. What have you given up believing at this point? Is that really the truth? What is another way to look at it?

3. What positive efforts from your partner have you disregarded or ignored recently? How would that make you feel? How do you think it makes them feel?

4. Do you believe your partner cares enough about you to want to change and why?

5. Do you care enough about your partner to change and why?

6. What negative feelings will you no longer tolerate in your relationship?

7. What is worth fighting for in your relationship?

8. What negative feelings have you grown comfortable accepting in your life?

9. When things are great between you, what specifically has happened to make you feel special to each other?

10. What are ten things you love about your spouse?

11. What are three actions you could take right now to improve your relationship?

12. Before you call it quits, can you look your partner in the eyes and honestly tell them you don't love them anymore and know in your soul that is the truth?

13. Before you call it quits, if you could have your partner understand your deepest hurt, sadness or fear, what would that be?

14. What are you afraid to share with your mate that keeps you at odds with each other?

15. What could you try before walking away that might make things a lot better? What else could you try? What else?

16. What do you really want that you're not getting? Have you asked yourself what your partner wants that they are not getting from you?

3

the power of decision

O ne of the best ways to ensure that you're doing whatever it takes to change the energy of your relationship is to fully appreciate and exercise the power of decision. Every decision you have ever made in your life is a chain of events that has led you to where you are today. This awesome power determines the course of your life. The incredible thing is how swiftly decisions can be made and how much impact even seemingly small decisions have on your life. Just think, **how many little decisions have resulted in whether you're ecstatically happy in your relationship or whether you're totally miserable**?

If you traced every decision back to how you feel about your relationship currently, you'd see that often each little one builds on the last to completely change the quality and direction of your life. If at every interaction with your partner you habitually decide to be impatient, cold, controlling, selfish, angry, or judgmental, can you see how that can create momentum that can spiral toward extreme feelings of sadness, hurt, frustration, disconnection, anger or loneliness? The reverse is true, too. You can consistently decide to express love instead of indifference. When your spouse hasn't responded to you in a way that you expected, you can decide to be patient rather than frustrated and angry. Each new interaction will build trust and nurture the intimacy between you.

The toughest decision unhappy couples are faced with is whether or not to give up the fight. If all of your time together is spent arguing or in total silence in separate rooms, eventually you become so dissatisfied that something has to give. If you are at the point in your life where you feel like you're roommates at best, we feel for you. We also applaud you because if you're reading this book it means you're still searching for answers. The best encouragement we can offer, if both of you are truly committed to your love and are interested in finding a solution to what seems unsolvable, is the resources are available to learn how to change.

You don't have to look too far these days to find statistics that tell you how often people exhausted by their search for answers decide to end their relationships. The divorce statistics are staggering in this country and abroad.

The most tragic situations are couples with young children whose lives will forever be altered by the break up of their mother and father. There are certainly great examples of children who rise above being the product of divorced parents and couples who have moved on to more fulfilling lives separately than they would have had together. For every one of those exceptions, there are far more examples of people who will carry deep feelings of regret, sadness, guilt and failure for years as a result of their decision that divorce or separation were their only alternatives.

If you have children , our hope is you will believe in the possibility of transforming your lives together until you actually have that moment of insight that puts it all together for you. It may not happen immediately, but the examples are available to follow if you look long and hard enough.

Ultimately what will determine whether you continue seeking a more fulfilling way to live is what you have determined it is worth to you. What would it be worth to know that you can clarify the root cause of your relationship problems? What would life be like if daily you were in a place of joy and happiness? How long would you look to find how to shorten the painful moments with your partner and lengthen the enjoyable ones? How peaceful would it feel to know that you didn't have to break up your family; that you could actually bring harmony to your family life and have the intimacy you desire with your mate at the same time? The decision is yours. Will you stop the search and settle for a life far less than you deserve or will you persist until you have recreated the relationship of your hearts desire?

We were faced with the same decision two years ago. We were as close as you get to breaking up our family with two young children to consider. We were feeling desperately at odds with each other and paralyzed by the fear of making the wrong decision. The one thing we did decide to do is continue to search for the reason why relationships die.

Fortunately for us and our family we found the answers we were looking for. It was not an easy path to travel. It involved exerting the power of decision to do whatever it would take to get clear on how to live as the loving couple we knew in our hearts we once were. The experience was literally priceless: it gave us hearts full of love for each other and the self respect that comes from knowing we hung in long enough to take our relationship in a completely different direction.

The next chapter describes what we experienced that created such an extraordinary breakthrough. May this be equally eye opening for you and your partner.

Questions to Ponder | *Chapter 3: Power of Decision*

1. What are some decisions you've made that you're certain have had a negative impact on your relationship?

2. What are some decisions that had obviously positive effects on your relationship?

3. What have you decided to value more than improving your connection together?

4. Have you decided that you will do whatever it takes to find answers to your problems?

5. What is the one big decision you could make to shift momentum toward each other instead of away from each other?

6. What are some "little things" you've decided aren't important enough to do anymore?

7. What would happen if you started noticing the "little things" your partner does for you?

8. What would happen if you started doing the "little things" again?

9. What is the next step you need to decide to take to improve the quality of your lives together?

10. If you decided to believe that lasting change was possible, how would that change efforts in your relationship? What would you do differently?

11. If you decided to end your relationship, what would you regret not giving? What if you decided to give it and see what happens?

12. Is there a decision you are afraid to make for fear of losing the love of your partner? If so, what is it?

our change of heart

In an effort to improve the quality of our lives together during our marital problems, we attended seminars, read books, listened to CDs, and watched television shows geared toward developing relationship and life skills to break through problems. Any one of the skills we learned could have significantly helped us if we weren't so consumed by the fear of facing the truth of what was really going on in our marriage. All the education was valuable. Even though we weren't using what we learned, it dripped on us like a leaky faucet pushing us toward facing the truth. The fact that we were continuously miserable was a clear indication we still needed work in this area of our lives.

Our efforts to find answers ultimately paid off with the loving support of some close family members who offered us tickets to yet another seminar. This one was quite different, however. In December of 2003, we attended an Anthony Robbins live seminar in the Bahamas. From the very beginning we could feel that this was our opportunity to finally get clear on what was really going on in our relationship and work on lasting solutions. The event was packed with content related to understanding why people experience the emotions they do on a daily basis and how to design your emotional life to support your fulfillment. One particularly powerful piece of this multi-day event was Robbins' description of the five elements of the chemistry of transformation.

He related that no one will ever make lasting change until they first get satiated with whatever circumstance in their life is bothering them such as a relationship problem. Once you get satiated and know in your gut you've had enough you will reach dissatisfaction. As you begin to focus on your dissatisfaction you will reach an emotional threshold where what used to be comfortable is no longer okay. At that threshold, you will be at the point where an insight is possible. When you get an insight, there is a brief window of momentum to transform. It is at that point that you need to take advantage of the opportunity to change. If you shrink back out of fear of the unknown or the discomfort of letting go of your problem, the window of built up emotion closes and you go back indefinitely to living with your problem until you get satiated again.

As the seminar concluded for the day, "The Chemistry of Transformation" segment resonated with us because we were so satiated and dissatisfied with our life's circumstances. As the next day of content began, we were feeling at a threshold with our relationship; it was no longer okay to live as disconnected, lonely people anymore. Our insight was the fleeting power of overwhelming dissatisfaction. We didn't want to miss our opportunity to tap in to the resources available for change at this seminar. We stepped through our window to transform.

In front of a room filled with four thousand people we stood up in the aisle of the seminar and asked Anthony Robbins for his guidance to solve our marital problems. There we stood for over two hours as Mr. Robbins deciphered the components of what was tearing us apart. We were fortunate to have close relatives with us at the event who also stood up and provided valuable insights to Mr. Robbins with their perspective on why we were so unhappy together. As we worked with Robbins directly, he compassionately held an emotional mirror in front of us, which showed us the specific patterns of behavior we had engaged in that resulted in our painful life together. For our benefit and the benefit of all the seminar participants, he masterfully blended the metaphor of our relationship with the tools to create lasting change. At the end of our time together the truth of our real love for each other was evident. We made an emotional shift to a totally different world together that changed both of us to our core. It became obvious that the common themes in our relationship were also common to struggling relationships in general. We learned there are specific reasons why relationships begin to die.

Using Robbins' tools you can counteract years of negative conditioning if you are willing to face the truth and are committed to your partner.

Questions to Ponder | *Chapter 4: Our Change of Heart*

1. What are some reasons you believe your relationship is dying?

2. What is it that you are so fed up with you would do anything to change in your relationship?

3. What are your expectations for affection, respect, consideration, honesty, fun, spontaneity? How do you communicate your expectations?

4. Is your current state of your relationship living up to your expectations in these important areas? What other areas do you feel are important to your relationship?

5. What are you disappointed about in yourself?

6. What are you disappointed with your partner about?

5

why relationships die -
meeting each other's needs

Why is it that some relationships continually grow while others start out great and gradually lose their energy? There are a lot of different circumstances and personalities within relationships which make each one completely unique. This could make finding a common answer difficult. However, looking instead at what is similar provides useful clues.

One of the biggest similarities of relationships is they all involve the needs of human beings. Anthony Robbins developed the study of Human Needs Psychology which looks deeper into this reality. Human Needs Psychology asserts that all people have six core human needs. They are:

1. **Certainty / Comfort:** The ability to produce, eliminate or avoid stress; or the ability to create, increase or intensify pleasure.

2. **Uncertainty/Variety:** The need for surprise, diversity, difference, excitement, or challenge.

3. **Significance:** A sense of being needed, a feeling of importance, a sense of purpose, uniqueness, or sense of meaning.

4. **Love/Connection:** A need for bonding, oneness, sharing, intimacy, feeling at one with, or feeling a part of.

5. **Growth:** A spiritual need if you are to feel truly fulfilled in life.

6. **Contribution:** Also a spiritual need that leads to greater fulfillment in life.

It is important to understand that these needs are must haves in life—they are not wants. People have a deep seated drive within themselves to meet these needs in order to survive emotionally. Further, there are many unique ways that each individual meets their needs called **vehicles**. These vehicles can be destructive, neutral, or constructive in their effect on an individuals emotional and physical condition.

Some examples of common vehicles are:

- **Certainty:** Seeking control or consistency, learned helplessness, completion of tasks or projects, having faith.

- **Uncertainty/variety:** Use of alcohol, food, drugs, new job, learning, new relationship.

- **Significance:** Tearing others down, material possessions, accomplishments, having children, violence, growing levels of caring about others.

- **Love/Connection:** Sympathy through sickness or injury, commit a negative act (crime, drugs, smoking),gangs, spirituality, relationships, self sacrifice, beauty, sex.

For many people, a relationship is the most powerful vehicle that allows them to meet all six of their needs at a very high level, when handled properly. A relationship can be a total nightmare if you begin to find it difficult to meet your needs within it. Often, couples starting a relationship find it easy to meet their own needs and help their partner meet theirs.

Trouble arises over time if the partners injure the relationship whether by assuming the worst of the other, being manipulative, judgmental, abusive, betraying trust, or rejecting displays of affection. What each partner learns is that it's too painful to spend any length of time relating to their mate so they stop trying to meet their needs within the relationship and consequently stop giving to their partner. As the pain of not relating to each other increases, couples who still must meet their six human needs will seek other vehicles outside the relationship in an attempt to feel the same level of fulfillment.

The problem with this approach is that there is no vehicle that can deliver the same level of emotional intensity. Can you think of anything better to invest your life's energy into than a growing, loving, passionate relationship? So when the partners spend more and more time meeting their needs outside their relationship, they settle for a lot less intimacy, love, and connection with their mate. They will tend to find comfort, certainty, and significance elsewhere and the relationship will cease to grow. At that point, partners will not be contributing to each other and will start wondering or questioning why they are still together.

Understanding human needs and their role in a satisfying relationship can be a complex issue at first. We were completely confused about how to meet each other's needs. Our approach was hit or miss, like we were throwing darts in the dark shooting for a bull's eye we couldn't see. With this approach it should be no surprise that we found it difficult to help each other feel love and happiness in our marriage. Have you ever felt like no matter how you tried to improve your relationship it didn't seem to make things better? The following real life example will help you see how misunderstanding each other's needs leads to frustration and unnecessary pain.

A battle of wills developed early in our relationship. We both have strong personalities, so many times our discussions resulted in intense disagreements. Our disagreements commonly involved how to balance time with our extended families. My wife felt that she was tolerated but not truly accepted by some of my family, so naturally she wasn't excited about spending time with them. I felt we spent too much time with her family and not enough with mine, which led me to choose sides.

Can you see how this can be a no-win situation if you don't handle it well? Someone is going to get hurt and both sides were forcing a choice. I chose to sacrifice the relationship I had with my family. I gave up fighting because I wanted harmony and love in my marriage, but, in turn, stopped expressing my true feelings.

This strategy ended up backfiring on me. Soon my habit was to please or appease my wife rather than speak my mind. That choice had the consequence of weakening me emotionally. My weakness caused us to be disconnected and I began to resent being in the middle. If I understood my wife's needs, I would have known that by resisting or acting indifferent to spending time with my family, my wife was really trying to give me a clue how to meet her needs better.

She was trying to say that she didn't feel **love and connection** with me because I allowed my family's indifference to her to persist. She didn't feel that she was **significant** enough for me to take a stand with my family to stop it. She didn't feel **certain or comfortable** that I was a strong enough man to confront it. She also felt a lack of **certainty** or **comfort** that she would be accepted by them if we spent time with them. I could have helped her feel **significance, love, and connection** by seeking to understand rather than argue. I could have helped her feel more **certainty** by persisting in bridging the emotional gap she felt with me and my family.

My wife misunderstood my needs as well. I didn't want to sacrifice **love, connection,** and **significance** with her or with my family. I loved them both. Her resistance was causing me to choose. Also, by preferring to spend more time with her family, she showed me that they were more **significant** to her than my feelings. Rather than resisting and avoiding my family, she could have chosen to work with me to resolve the conflicts, which would have helped me feel more **significant** to her and more **love**.

Mr. Robbins brought clarity to why problems like this one continually arose in our marriage. He helped us figure out the two needs we were each trying to meet most often in our relationship and their order of importance to us. When we understood that critical piece it helped us recognize how our consistent behavior intensified our negative feelings about our marriage.

For my wife, feeling **certainty** that she would be loved by me and provided for financially was most important at the time. Feeling **love** and giving love was a very close second. My need for feeling **significant** to her was first. Receiving and giving **love** was a very close second. We learned by valuing **certainty** more than **love** my wife couldn't allow herself to feel **love** or give it when she felt **uncertain.** We also learned that when I didn't feel **significant** to her, I would pull **love** away. If you value any other need higher than love in a relationship you will be headed for a lot of pain—it's only a matter of time. Our relationship degenerated over time because neither of us was meeting the needs we conditioned ourselves to value most, so our love didn't flow back and forth.

As we mentioned earlier, it's predictable when two people are starving for love from each other and value other needs higher that aren't being met in the relationship, they will go outside of their relationship and use other vehicles to meet their needs. That is exactly what we did. Our importance to each other became clouded by stacked hurts and emotionally distancing ourselves.

I sought significance through burying myself in work and telling myself someday I would leave my troubled marriage where I wasn't appreciated. I would also reinforce my own significance by regarding myself as more physically fit than my wife; in effect judging her for not taking better care of herself.

My wife sought to meet her need for certain love by focusing her attention on our kids. She was also 100 percent certain she would get love from her family, so she reversed the importance of our marriage with a stronger connection to her family. During our periods of financial uncertainty she would seek money from her family so she could feel comfortable that we would be able to maintain our lifestyle.

We were able to make a shift in our values when we realized that not valuing love first and foremost in our lives set us up to always be searching for ways to feel fulfilled outside of our marriage. Once we reprioritized love over certainty and significance, we naturally felt more certainty and significance in our marriage. We felt much more fulfillment together. Our relationship became our primary vehicle to meet our needs together and our old vehicles diminished in importance.

If you can identify what your partner's top two needs are, in what order they value them, and how exactly they're meeting them, you have an opportunity to deliver what they need as long as you truly care about doing so. If you can learn to meet your partner's top two needs, you can rebuild a connection with each other that can be the foundation for growing the relationship. Eventually, you'll be able to mutually meet all of each other's needs as you grow together.

1. What are ways that you feel your relationship has been injured?

2. Where do you spend time or energy outside of your relationship to meet your needs?

3. What needs would you say you currently value most?

4. What needs do you believe are most important to your partner?

5. How would your partner say you could meet their needs better?

6. Are you willing to accept 100 percent honest feedback from your partner regarding strengths and weakness in your relationship?

7. What are some ways your mate communicates with you that makes you feel disconnected?

8. How would you like your partner to communicate to make you feel more loved and what specifically would they say?

6

giving your gifts

If you choose to value love as your highest need, you will find that you naturally will want to give to your partner. You'll want to figure out what contribution you can make that will grow the level of connection, intimacy, and attraction between you. We found that learning what specifically enhances femininity in a woman and masculinity in a man allowed us to understand our most important gifts to each other. Making that shift dramatically improved our relationship. Once we learned where to focus our attention we were set up for growing levels of fulfillment in our marriage.

Whether he admits it or not, a man lives to make his woman happy. When he makes her happy he feels successful. He feels more like a man. There are times, however, when no matter what a man gives it isn't enough. This makes him feel like a failure and less of a man. If he indulges feelings of rejection he will often pull love away from her because he doesn't feel like she appreciates his efforts. Has this situation ever occurred in your relationship? It was too common in ours before we became aware of what was missing.

When I couldn't figure out how I could make my wife happy I often would check out through reading, watching TV or going to work. Things became silent around the house. I didn't put in any further effort figuring it wasn't going to change how she felt. I gave her no attention at all. My approach made sense to me, but I was lonelier and my wife seemed unhappier. I needed to learn how I was showing up in my marriage. It was not only not masculine, it was counterproductive to helping my wife give her gift to me. A man's truly masculine gift is to allow his woman to feel his strength that comes in many forms. One of the biggest demonstrations of strength is to show her that his love will never be pulled away. When a woman knows that she can rely on her man's strength, she feels safe in his love for her and she can feel free to open her heart. When her heart is open, she can give her gift fully to him by showering him with love, appreciating his efforts to make her happy, and making him the number one priority in her life.

The concept is simple in theory. It seems all a man has to do is allow his woman to feel his love consistently and a woman simply needs to make her man number one in her life. It is not exactly that simple, in practice. Men and woman commonly misunderstand the messages of masculine and feminine energy they continually send each other. Men usually misunderstand that feminine energy in a woman will cause her to naturally test her man's strength all the time. When a man fails a woman's test for strength, she will feel uncertain that she can trust him with her open heart and true feelings.

This was the case in our marriage. When my wife was feeling uncertain about how much I loved her, she would withdraw from me to see if I got the message that she needed to feel more of my love. She wanted me to pursue her to show more interest in loving her. I took her withdrawal literally as not making her happy and rejecting me. When I felt rejected, I withdrew even further from her. What that taught her is that I was not strong enough to pass the test and figure out her need for love. She responded by closing down her heart out of the fear of being un-loved. Strictly from the uncertainty of not feeling my love, she began to behave in a controlling way to meet her need for certainty and fill the void of strength in the marriage. The last thing she wanted to be was controlling. She wanted my love but felt powerless to attract it. She attempted to control it with her own strength so she could feel some level of love from me. If I had realized that feminine energy thrives on attention and given her more of it, she wouldn't have felt the need to shift into control.

When women seek to control a man's love, they are misunderstanding two vitally important aspects of masculine energy. A man interprets an attempt to control and manipulate a relationship as a challenge. Masculine energy thrives on chal-lenge, but there is nothing attractive about a battle for control. Both partners will assume a more masculine energy and there will be a loss of polarity or difference in the relationship. Attraction only grows as the amount of difference between the partner's energies grows. If both partners take on the same energy, there will be a natural loss of attraction to each other. Women have all the power they will ever need by simply making sure their love is focused on their man before anyone else even their children. The reason for this is because a woman who gives herself fully to her partner makes him feel how important he is to her and how happy she is. Remember, a man lives to make his woman happy and there is no greater expression of happiness than for a woman to focus her love on her man. When she does, she owns his devoted soul. Can there possibly be anything more powerful?

If you are currently feeling unappreciated or unloved it is understandable that you would feel apprehensive about embracing these ideas. It wouldn't be uncommon to continue with your comfortable ways of feeling appreciated or loved through work, hobbies, friends or kids. None of those avenues will enable you to feel the intimacy that you crave with your partner.

With a new appreciation of the most important gifts to give each other you can better choose how to focus your energy. It can start by simply giving each other a few minutes of uninterrupted time at the end of a day to connect. If a man starts to express genuine interest in how his partner's day went and is willing to give her his undistracted presence, she will be able to unload her daily burdens and fill up again with his love.

This accomplishes two important outcomes: it gives a woman the attention her feminine core needs, and shows her she can trust that her man truly cares enough to understand her. Too often in conversation with their partners, men have a tendency to want to find the problem and fix it so they can be done with it and relax. It is part of the masculine nature to seek solutions to problems and rise above challenges. The problem is women don't want to be fixed; they want to be understood. To truly understand, men have to take the focus off how to solve the problem and more on listening so their women can release what is blocking their flow of love. We learned a fantastic metaphor that helped us understand feminine energy better.

Women are like storms of emotion. They express the broad spectrum of how they feel. Sometimes they don't fully understand why they feel the way they do, so a man's effort to fix what is not clearly defined can be frustrating. Don't resist the storm of emotion. It will only last longer. The storm will pass only when a woman feels understood.

I remember one time my wife and I were conversing, we disagreed or snipped at everything each other said. Eventually, I got frustrated and said, "This is going nowhere. Let's just agree not to talk to each other for a while." That was not well received, but rather than continue to bicker with her I chose to sit next to her, be quiet and hold her in my arms. I said nothing for about two or three minutes. Suddenly, she started crying and related that she missed her dad. I decided to stop fighting the storm. In turn, she was able to open up and mourn the fairly recent loss of her father. It was interesting that I perceived her mood as being disagreeable. Sometimes your perception of someone's feelings is not at all what is really bothering them. There are occasions when a man's seemingly small gift of a quiet and strong presence makes all the difference in allowing a woman to open up to express her real feelings.

Women can give back to their men in small ways that make a big difference as well. When a woman is genuinely happy to see her man at the end of the day, his eyes will light up every time he sees her. The more often she is excited to see him when he gets home, gradually, he will feel more appreciated. When a woman takes her focus off of her need to unload all the frustrations of the day and takes a moment to energetically welcome her man home, he will definitely feel it and naturally want to be fully present for her to express her feelings. Sometimes it can be as simple as greeting him at the door with a smile and a loving look in her eye.

As appreciating and understanding each other becomes a habit, partners begin to look forward to the end of the day to reconnect with each other and their relationship becomes a desirable place to come back to. When we were in the midst of feeling disconnected from each other, we remember how much we dreaded coming home. We had no appreciation for each other and made no effort to understand one another's daily struggles. We found that the habit of acknowledging each other immediately on returning home fed our energy and strengthened our bond. Our children even noticed the difference. They began to feel the connection growing as we changed our habits. As parents we are now modeling sincere expressions of love that influence our children in a much more positive way. Can you see how these small changes begin to shift the tide in a relationship?

Questions to Ponder | *Chapter 6: Giving your Gifts*

1. When have you pulled love away from your partner and what happened to make you do that?

2. How have you "checked out" in your relationship believing nothing will ever change? What would happen if you chose to give more of your natural gifts?

3. How have you tested your partner? When you have tested, how has your partner reacted/responded?

4. What are some things your partner could do or say that would increase the feelings of devotion you would feel?

5. How often are the things that seem to be the problem, not really the problem at all? How do you handle it? What could you do or say to uncover the truth of what is really going on?

6. Have you asked yourself what the problem looks like from your partner's perspective?

sustaining transformation

Our intervention shed light on our previous behaviors and beliefs. Once we learned that our behaviors were driven by our beliefs, and became aware of which beliefs were destroying our relationship, we had new hope for sustainable change in our marriage. We learned what not to allow space for in our lives. This fostered optimism for a much brighter future together. With a new perspective, we could now see how many emotional land mines we set up for ourselves, what we did to trip them, and more importantly, how to avoid them all together. We had a map to guide us in making new choices of what thoughts and emotions to reinforce in the future. That shift in focus made us more acute to a set of values we have found to be the core strengths of our relationship today.

We hope sharing our values will leave some clues to navigate the minefield of emotional pain that a troubled relationship can be. Our greatest wish is that our marriage can be both a warning and an example for your relationship. We realize every couple has a unique chemistry to their lives together. What is important to us may not be as important to you. Still, we can't help but notice the glaring difference that emphasizing these values has made in our lives since our intervention. Our perspective may seem too simple. You may feel like we are not telling you anything you don't already know. We have found in our own relationship that doing and knowing are two completely different experiences. The simplicity in no way diminishes the power to enrich your lives together. What has made all the difference for us is an uncompromising devotion to our realigned value system and an intolerance for allowing the behaviors of the past to consistently manifest themselves.

It is not like we are living in a fantasy land; we still have real life situations that test our resolve to make our bond the primary focus of our lives. What we have done is realized the consistent expression of love as our core value. The key for our ability to feel love flowing back and forth particularly in stressful times is making it easy to feel. In the past we had too many ideas of what needed to happen before we would allow ourselves to give or receive love. We focused far too much on what we were missing from each other. When your thoughts, words and deeds are centered around what your partner isn't or doesn't do there is no space for loving feelings. We feel this is at the heart of why many couples feel so alone.

At this point in our lives when we have moments where we pull love away from each other or times when we are not making each other number one it feels like we are touching a hot stove. We have clearly learned the destructive effect of indulging selfishness or withholding our gifts from each other. When this happens, we stop and ask ourselves if this is really the way we want to feel toward each other. Is it more important to be right or to indulge your frustration? The answer always comes back to wanting to feel more love. A simple step in keeping our emotions in check is being willing to deal quickly with what is causing the upset in the moment rather than letting upset fester and build into resentment. We are now clear that pulling love away is no longer an option regardless of how upset we may be. We are human and sometimes delude ourselves that it feels better to be angry or frustrated, but our hearts know the truth.

our values and beliefs

forgiveness

Love will not flourish in your lives if you're still holding onto painful feelings and regarding your partner as the primary reason for those feelings. There is no peace without forgiveness. True forgiveness is where you both forgive and forget anything that has come between you. Heartfelt forgiveness is a huge gift to a relationship. If you insist on keeping a mental rolodex of things your partner did or didn't do in the past to hurt you, you will relive the pain over and over and will be easier to justify anger toward your mate. When you release the pain, both of you elevate the energy of your bond to the higher energy of love. When love replaces the space of resentment in your heart, the pain dies and you can experience the wonderful life you dream about. Stop believing that you have to give yourself time to forgive. **Forgiveness happens in one instant and when it happens, you unlock the power to fulfill your dreams together.** The habit of apologizing even for little things you know were inconsiderate toward your mate shows that you value each other.

Forgiveness did not come easy to us in the past because we were more focused on keeping score and justifying our unhappiness with each other.

living the truth

A big piece of the enlightenment we have experienced comes from an appreciation for living what is true in our lives, good or bad, and using it to grow our relationship. When two people aren't allowing full expression of real feelings between each other distance will grow. One or both of you aren't being who you really are. The relationship then becomes based on a false sense of who you believe you need to be to live up to the expectations of the other whether real or imagined.

Daring to live authentically is another value we have embraced that has brought peace to our lives. Living authentically involves being consistently open to the risk of being judged, shamed, hurt or feeling inadequate for the love of your partner. When real love exists between two people, these fears are an illusion built up from the anxiety of being totally vulnerable to another person. When you witness each other living authentically you can't help but nurture an overwhelming respect for one another because it takes courage to be honest, and courage is universally admirable.

When you are living the truth and are not made wrong by your partner for being compassionately honest or expressing all of who you are, it builds a trust of safety to continue the same way of relating to each other. You're planting seeds of growth in your bond together. With trust and respect as a foundation, you now experience growing levels of intimacy. Isn't intimacy what we are truly crave when we seek to spend our lives with someone? Don't we want to be able to bare our souls to each other and feel appreciated and loved for who we really are? It is possible to create a relationship with that level of depth, but first you must decide that living emotionally in the gray middle ground isn't enough anymore. When you realize how empty living numb makes you feel and let that feeling resonate to the core of your soul, you begin to wake internally to a knowing that more is possible. Ask yourself, Is this really what a loving relationship should feel like? You will start feeling the truth that you deserve more than what you've settled for. Intense love, passion, caring, playfulness or whatever emotions you feel are missing are yours for the asking when you decide you must have them in your life.

When you approach the threshold of living the truth you may feel a crush of doubts about taking the next step to express your true self. You may begin to doubt that you have the inner strength that it takes to manifest what your heart desires. If you allow the doubts to control your behavior, it's likely that you will lose the emotional momentum you've created. This is your pivotal point in the process of claiming your destiny together. What have you been withholding about who you are or what you value that makes you feel like you're living life smaller than you know in your heart you truly deserve? A decision to accept the familiarity of what has always been is a decision to go on living a false life together. Is that really what you want?

antedote to doubts

The polar opposite of doubt is faith. We would be remiss if we didn't articulate the degree to which valuing faith in times of massive doubt and confusion has transformed our lives. When you believe strongly that you have reached the end of your rope and a break up is inevitable, it's time for deep soul searching. We found in those moments that nurturing a belief that there are no coincidences in life, that we were guided to be together and would be guided through hard times, made all the difference.

The capacity to trust in a power greater than you who knows nothing but love and wants nothing but what is best for you gives you the emotional strength to push yourself beyond what you previously believed you were capable of. We realize faith is a touchy subject for many people. Often, a discussion of faith gets people hung up on whether they believe in God, in which God they believe, or if they even call It God. The bottom line is there are aspects of faith that you need to embrace if you are to have a breakthrough in your relationship. We believe it starts and ends with a heartfelt knowing that you will always be loved by your Creator because you were created from love, so you can risk being unloved by another person. You can never lose the love of your Creator if you remember that your very life is a gift of love.

So go ahead and face whatever is holding you back from feeling the way that you want to feel. Have the faith to know that you can withstand possible rejection and the withdrawal of love from your partner. Express yourself fully and you may experience the exact opposite reaction from your mate than you might expect. You may find a love and respect that you have never felt before.

In the time that has past since our intervention, we have found that giving each other the benefit of the doubt by not assuming the worst of each other is another expression of faith. When you assume the worst you hurt your partner and consequently the whole relationship. We have accessed our ability to have faith in each other when on the surface our behavior seemed to resemble the "old us." By one of us not engaging the old behavior and hanging in there believing that the other would come around quickly put an end to the potentially destructive energy. If you lose faith in each other when things seem to be going backwards, you start moving toward questioning the relationship. If you take this approach you weaken the bond and halt the progress you have made together.

appreciation

Create an urgency within yourself to notice the beauty in your life that is right beside you, or chances are you could get to the end of your life wondering why you never experienced the fulfillment you desired from your relationship. Do you really want to live life reacting to everything around you rather than allowing yourself to feel how much you are loved and what your partner means to the quality of your life? We all have to get to our next appointment, pick the kids up, or whatever demands of the day capture your attention.

Stop. Take thirty seconds to sincerely appreciate all you are given by your soul mate. Once you notice the beauty of what you've been given, how much your partner does for you and means to you, your life shifts in the blink of an eye. You must make it a priority to focus on gratitude. If you can find it in your heart to be grateful for the littlest thing that your partner does or says, you can't simultaneously feel what is missing and if you make gratitude an emotional habit you can't get to the place inside yourself where you habitually reinforce the belief that life would be better without your mate.

Questions to Ponder | *Chapter 7: Sustaining Transformation*

1. What are you finished allowing space for in your life that doesn't serve your relationship?

2. What has to happen in order for you to feel love in your relationship?

3. How long do you let things fester in your relationship? Explain how you can prevent this from continuing to happen.

4. What do you wish to be forgiven for and what do you want to forgive your partner for?

5. Describe who you are emotionally in your relationship. Who do you want to be? What three to six emotions do you most want to feel in your relationship? What emotions would you guess your partner wants to feel?

6. What have you settled for in your relationship? What are you no longer willing to settle for?

7. Are you in touch with a feeling of being guided spiritually regarding your relationship? If so, what direction do you feel is truthfully the way you need to go?

8. When and how do you give your partner the benefit of the doubt, and how has it changed the outcome?

9. What are some wonderful ways your partner has added to the quality of your life?

10. What are you grateful for in your relationship?

11. What are three of the most important areas in which you want to grow your relationship? Who do you have to become in order to nurture the growth?

12. How can you encourage your mate to grow with you?

summing it all up

If you are facing the possibility of ending your relationship or if you were just looking for ways to break out of an emotional rut hopefully the insights we have shared have created some shifts in the perceptions you have held about your options to this point. Ultimately the magnitude of progress you make related to the ideas we have expressed is determined by what you choose to do with the information provided. Sometimes resisting concepts that make us uncomfortable or not fully trusting what clearly works impedes a breakthrough in our lives. Have we given you reason to trust that things can be radically different for you as well? If so, we encourage you to take the next step. If you are on the verge of facing the truth of whether or not your relationship is built to last, don't hold anything back. Express yourself fully, become totally vulnerable to what lies ahead for you. Embrace the uncertainty that you don't know what will happen next. You will feel more alive than you have in a long time. Leap and the net will appear.